Grandma

"A loving heart is the truest wisdom."
 CHARLES DICKENS

For _____

From _____

The story of your life...🌷

Your date and place of birth:

_____

_____

Who named you, and how was your name chosen?

_____

_____

_____

_____

_____

_____

Your parents' names, birthdates, and places of birth:

_____

_____

_____

_____

_____

_____

_____

_____

_____

Your brothers and sisters, oldest to youngest:

_____

_____

_____

_____

_____

_____

Your aunts and uncles:

_____

_____

_____

_____

_____

_____

Who were you closest with in your family?

_____

_____

_____

_____

_____

_____

_____

_____

_____

_____

Do you know anything about the history of our family?

How did we immigrate to this country? Where did we settle?

How did we get to where we are now?

Childhood...

What's your first memory?

🌷 **M**emories . . . the food of our childhood, food that meant love ♥.

What kind of child were you?

What is a special memory you have of your mother?

_____

_____

_____

_____

_____

_____

_____

_____

_____

_____

Mom

Tell me about your dad.

_____

_____

_____

_____

_____

_____

_____

_____

_____

_____

_____

_____

_____

_____

_____

_____

_____

DaD

Tell me what you remember about your grandparents.

What were your favorite childhood pastimes?

_____
_____
_____
_____
_____
_____
_____
_____
_____

Did you play games with your family? If so, what were your favorites?

_____
_____
_____
_____
_____
_____
_____
_____
_____

Family Fun

Who was the clown of your family?

_____

_____

_____

_____

_____

_____

_____

_____

What made you laugh?

_____

_____

_____

_____

_____

_____

_____

_____

_____ *You were sooooo funny!*

Did you have pets?

_____

_____

_____

_____

_____

_____

_____

Describe your bedroom. Did you share your room or have it all to yourself?

_____

_____

_____

_____

_____

_____

_____

_____

_____

_____

_____

Did you have a television? What shows did you like to watch?

What was your favorite thing to eat?

What was a special meal your mom or dad made for you?

♥ ♥ ♥ YUM

Tell me about a memorable party or celebration.

Did you help out around the house?

_____

_____

_____

_____

_____

_____

_____

Did you get an allowance?

_____

_____

_____

_____

_____

_____

_____

_____

_____

Who were your childhood friends?

_____

_____

_____

_____

_____

_____

_____

_____

Where did they live?

_____

_____

_____

_____

_____

_____

_____

_____

On the road between the houses of friends, grass does not grow. ♥

What was your neighborhood like?

What games did you play when you were little?

Describe a special toy. Who gave it to you? What made it so special?

Little
Me!

What were your favorite books?

_____

_____

_____

_____

_____

_____

What was your favorite kind of music? How did you listen to it?

_____

_____

_____

_____

_____

_____

_____

_____

_____

_____

_____

_____

What kinds of movies did you like? Who were your favorite movie stars?
Are there any movies from that time that you still love to this day?

Where did you go to school?

_____

_____

_____

_____

How did you get there?

_____

_____

_____

_____

_____

_____

_____

_____

_____

_____

_____

_____

_____

_____

_____

Did you like school? Did you participate in any special school events?

_____

_____

_____

_____

_____

_____

_____

_____

_____

School days

Which were your best subjects?

_____

_____

_____

_____

_____

_____

_____

Tell me about a special teacher you still remember.

_____

_____

_____

_____

_____

_____

_____

_____

_____

_____

_____

_____

What did you typically do after school?

What were the rules of the house? Curfews?

Are there any dreams from your childhood that you still remember?

What did you do during your summers?

_____

_____

_____

_____

_____

_____

_____

_____

_____

_____

_____

_____

_____

_____

_____

_____

_____

Did your family take trips together?

Tell me about your religious upbringing. What were some memorable events?

How did your family spend the holidays?

What were your favorite holiday foods?

_____

_____

_____

_____

_____

_____

_____

_____

_____

_____

_____

_____

_____

_____

_____

Will you share a favorite holiday recipe here?

Recipe for: _____

Serves: _____

IT'S NOT WHAT'S ON THE PLATES THAT MATTERS, IT'S WHAT'S ON THE CHAIRS.

Tell me a story about a holiday family gathering.

A house is made of walls & beams; a home is built with love & dreams.

Growing up...

What did you dream about while growing up?

_____

_____

_____

_____

_____

_____

_____

_____

_____

_____

_____

_____

_____

_____

_____

_____

_____

_____

_____

What did you think you would be when you grew up?

_____

_____

_____

_____

_____

_____

_____

_____

_____

_____

AIN'T LIFE GRAND?

Did you wear makeup? Or nail polish?

_____

_____

_____

_____

_____

_____

_____

Tickle-Me Pink

How did you fix your hair?

_____

_____

_____

_____

_____

_____

_____

_____

_____

_____

_____

_____

_____

_____

Describe a favorite outfit.

_____

_____

_____

_____

_____

_____

_____

_____

_____

_____

_____

_____

_____

_____

_____

_____

_____

_____

_____

_____

_____

_____

me again...

Did you like fashion magazines? What did you read for fun?

"All that mankind has done, thought or been:
it is in magic preservation, in the pages of books."
♥ THOMAS CARLYLE

What did you do for fun?

_____

_____

_____

_____

_____

_____

_____

_____

_____

_____

_____

_____

_____

_____

_____

_____

_____

_____

_____

_____

Who was your very best friend? What made you so close?

_____

_____

_____

_____

_____

_____

_____

Where'd you go, what'd you do, and who'd you see together?

_____

_____

_____

_____

_____

_____

_____

_____

_____

_____

_____

FOREVER FRIENDS

Tell me about a best friend adventure.

_____

_____

_____

_____

_____

_____

_____

_____

_____

_____

_____

Did you ever leave school with your friends without your parents' permission?

FRIENDS

If you did something that your parents didn't like, what were the consequences?

_____

_____

_____

_____

_____

_____

_____

_____

What did you do that flew under the radar?

_____

_____

_____

_____

_____

_____

_____

_____

_____

_____

_____

_____

Tell me about your first date: the who-what-where-when-and-why, all the basics. How old were you? Where did you go, and what did you wear? What did your parents have to say about all of this?

"*Love is friendship set to music.*"
Anonymous

What was the biggest thing you remember happening in our country when you were in high school?

_____

_____

_____

_____

_____

_____

_____

Did you pay attention to politics? What did you believe in then?

_____

_____

_____

_____

_____

_____

_____

_____

_____

_____

_____

What's the best thing that's been invented since you were younger?

_____

_____

_____

_____

_____

_____

_____

_____

_____

_____

_____

_____

_____

_____

_____

_____

_____

_____

_____

_____

_____

How old were you when you got your driver's license?

Who taught you how to drive?

_____

_____

_____

_____

_____

_____

_____

_____

Tell me a story about learning to drive.

_____

_____

_____

_____

_____

_____

_____

_____

_____

_____

_____

_____

Did you go on any road trips? Share a story about a teenage adventure.

All grown up...

What did you do after high school? Did you go to college?

_____

_____

_____

_____

_____

_____

_____

_____

_____

_____

OLDER
Me!

What was your first place like? Did you live alone?

HOME
SWEET
HOME

Did you like being on your own?

_____

_____

_____

_____

_____

_____

_____

_____

What did you miss about living with your parents?

_____

_____

_____

_____

_____

_____

_____

_____

_____

_____

_____

Did you cook? What did you make?

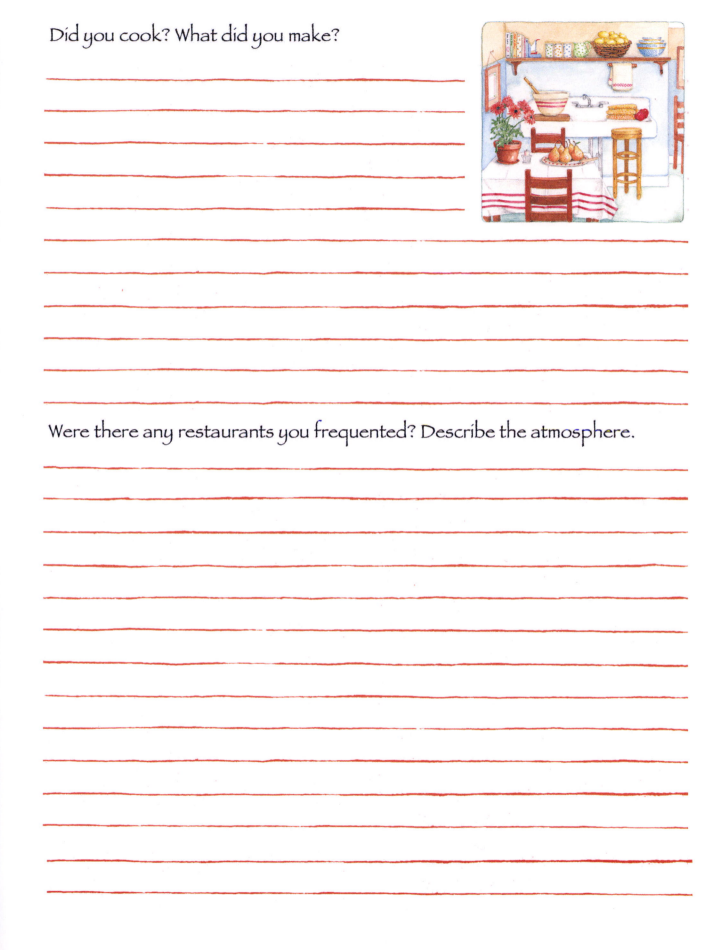

_____

_____

_____

_____

_____

_____

_____

Were there any restaurants you frequented? Describe the atmosphere.

_____

_____

_____

_____

_____

_____

_____

_____

_____

_____

What was your first job? How did you get it? Was it what you wanted to be doing?

_____

_____

_____

_____

_____

_____

_____

_____

_____

_____

_____

_____

_____

_____

_____

_____

_____

_____

"DO NOT PUT OFF TILL TOMORROW
WHAT CAN BE PUT OFF TILL
DAY AFTER TOMORROW JUST AS WELL."
♥ MARK TWAIN

What was your worst job ever? How long did you work there?

_____

_____

_____

_____

_____

_____

_____

If you could go back in time, what would you change about it?

_____

_____

_____

_____

_____

_____

_____

_____

_____

_____

Write a page or two about the loves of your life.

The love in your heart
wasn't put there to stay,
love isn't love
till it's
given
away.

With all your expertise, can you give your best advice about relationships?

Was there one who got away?

_____

_____

_____

_____

_____

_____

_____

_____

_____

_____

_____

_____

_____

_____

_____

_____

_____

_____

Did you ever fall in love at first sight?

(c o o)

LOVE BIRDS

YOU MAKE MY
HEART SING♪

What was the most romantic date you ever went on?

_____

_____

_____

_____

_____

_____

_____

_____

_____

_____

MR. WONDERFUL

Write about my grandfather and how you met him.
How has your relationship changed over the years?

Tell me about your first home together and having your first baby.
What year was that?

Did you enjoy being a mom?

What was your favorite thing?

What was my dad/mom like as a baby?

_____

_____

_____

_____

_____

_____

_____

_____

_____

_____

_____

_____

_____

_____

_____

_____

_____

_____

Tell a funny story about my parent as a child.

_____

_____

_____

_____

_____

_____

_____

_____

_____

_____

_____

_____

_____

_____

_____

_____

_____

_____

IF YOU DON'T WANT YOUR CHILDREN TO HEAR WHAT YOU'RE SAYING, PRETEND YOU'RE TALKING TO THEM. ♥ ANON.

Did you also work outside of the house? (How did you find the time!?)

What kinds of hobbies, activities, and vacations did you enjoy as a grown-up?

Where have you traveled that you loved best?

How did you spend your holidays when you had younger children?

_____

_____

_____

_____

_____

_____

_____

What are your favorite family traditions?

_____

_____

_____

_____

_____

_____

_____

_____

_____

_____

"Ah! There is nothing like Staying home for real comfort."
♥ JANE AUSTEN

When you heard you were going to be a grandma, how did you feel?
How old were you when I was born?

_____

_____

_____

_____

_____

_____

_____

_____

_____

_____

_____

_____

_____

_____

_____

_____

_____

_____

_____

Did you babysit for me?

What did we like to do, just the two of us?

_____

_____

_____

_____

_____

_____

_____

_____

_____

_____

_____

_____

_____

_____

_____

_____

_____

_____

Nobody can do for little children what grandmas do. Grandmas sprinkle STARDUST over lives of little children.

What are the differences between your children and grandchildren?

_____

_____

_____

_____

_____

_____

_____

_____

How are they similar?

_____

_____

_____

_____

_____

_____

_____

_____

_____

_____

_____

How has being a grandma been different than being a mom?

_____

_____

_____

_____

_____

_____

_____

_____

How has it been similar?

_____

_____

_____

_____

_____

_____

_____

_____

_____

_____

All about you...

What is the most surprising gift you have ever received?

_____

_____

_____

_____

_____

_____

_____

_____

_____

_____

_____

_____

_____

_____

_____

_____

_____

_____

_____

The best gifts are tied with heartstrings.

What's your secret food addiction?

_____

_____

_____

_____

_____

_____

_____

_____

_____

_____

_____

_____

_____

_____

_____

_____

_____

_____

All the things I really like to do are immoral, illegal, or fattening. ♥

What is a favorite family recipe of yours? Why is it special?

Will you write it down here?

Recipe for: _____

Serves: _____

SO GOOD ♥

What's your favorite quote, and why?

_____
_____
_____
_____
_____
_____
_____
_____

What's a favorite piece of jewelry that you own?

_____
_____
_____
_____
_____
_____
_____
_____
_____
_____
_____
_____

_____ THE BEST THINGS IN LIFE AREN'T THINGS. ♥

Who are your heroes?

What do you love to do?

If you could be any age, which would you choose?

_____

_____

_____

_____

_____

_____

_____

_____

_____

_____

_____

_____

_____

_____

_____

_____

_____

_____

_____

"Backward, turn backward, O Time in your flight;
Make me a child again just for tonight." ♥

Elizabeth Akers Allen

If you could do it all over again, would you change anything?

What hopes and dreams do you have for the future?

What would you most like to be remembered for?

_____

_____

_____

_____

_____

_____

_____

_____

_____

_____

_____

_____

_____

_____

_____

_____

_____

_____

_____

"Charm: the quality in others that makes us more satisfied with ourselves."

Henri-Frédéric Amiel

What is your best advice about life?

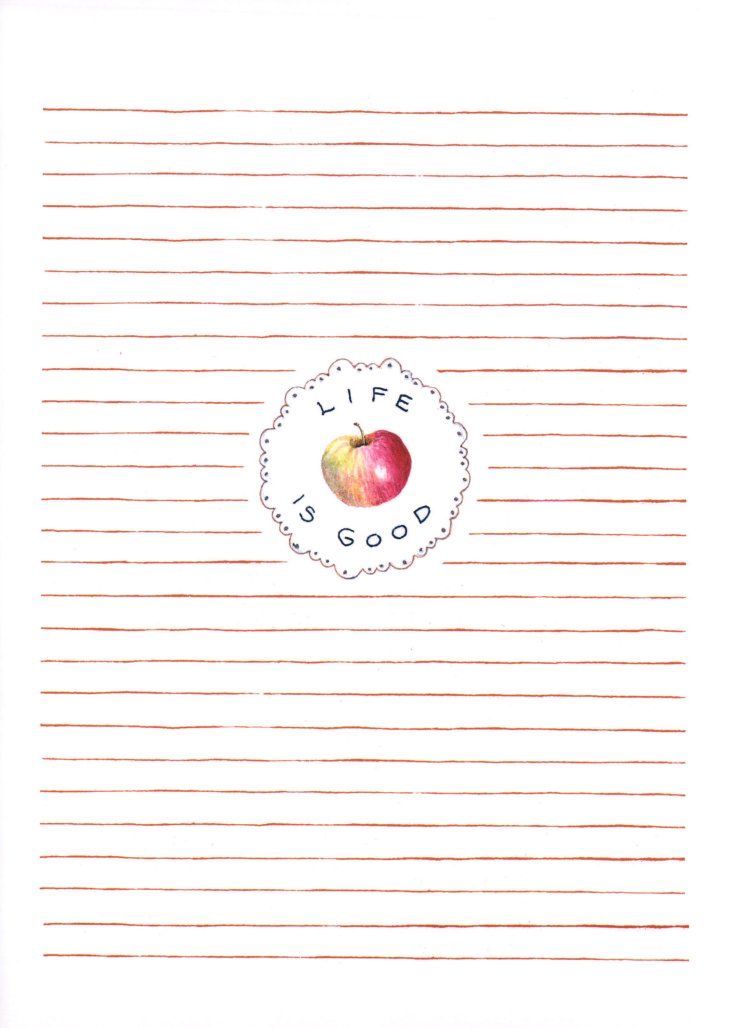

What makes you the happiest?

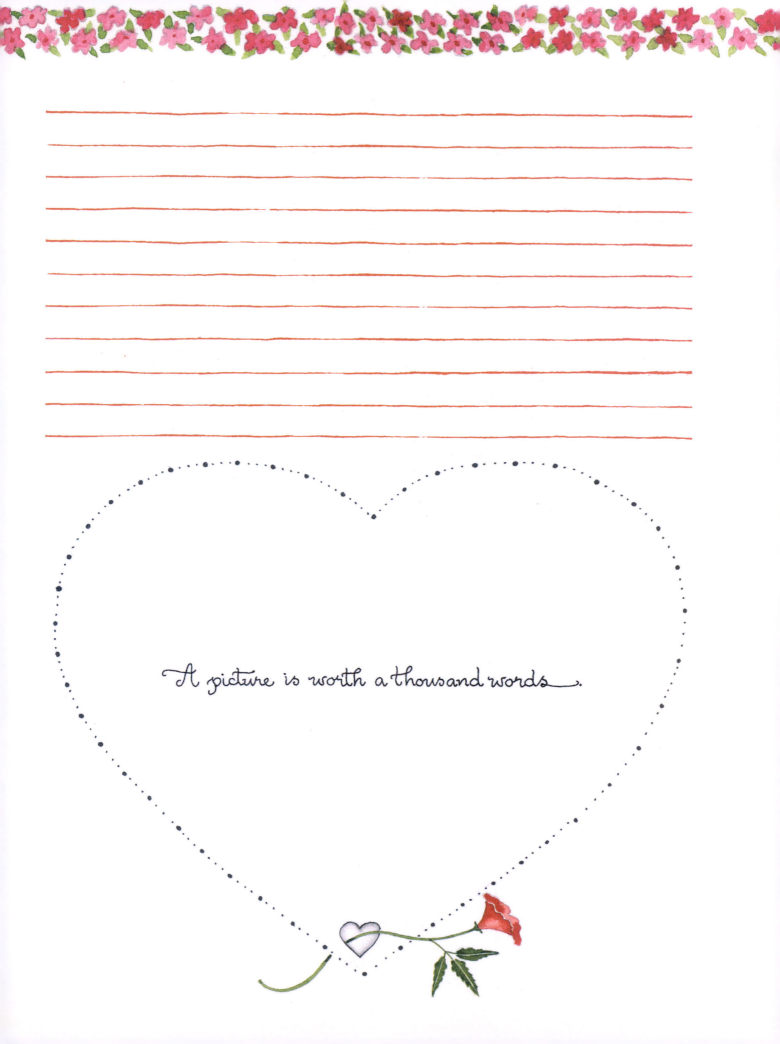

A picture is worth a thousand words.

What is the most important thing you have learned?

AIN'T LIFE GRAND?

Hours fly
Flowers die
New days
New ways
Pass by
Love stays

More stories...

Picture Perfect

memories

WHERE SHALL I BEGIN? WHICH OF MY IMPORTANT THINGS SHALL I TELL YOU FIRST? Jane Austen

Special Times

Great, wide, beautiful, wonderful World,
With the wonderful water round you curled,
And the wonderful grass upon your breast,
World, you are beautifully dressed.

♥ W. B. Rands

Precious Moments

A picture goes here;
your family, your house,
your dog, your cat —
but best would be
YOU
since this is your book. ♥

(THAT'S MY STORY & I'M STICKING TO IT!)

_____

My signature

_____

Date